# Anteaters

## By Sam Dollar

Steadwell
Books

Raintree Steck-Vaughn Publishers
A Harcourt Company

Austin · New York
www.steck-vaughn.com

ANIMALS OF THE RAIN FOREST

Published by Raintree Steck-Vaughn Publishers, an imprint of Steck-Vaughn Company.

**Library of Congress Cataloging-in-Publication Data**
Cataloging-in-Publication data is available upon request.


**Produced by Compass Books**

**Photo Acknowledgments**
Corbis/Tom Brakefield, 4-5, 20; George Lepp, 12; Michael & Patricia Fogden, cover, title page, 15, 22; Kevin Schafer, 16; Dave G. Houser, 28
Visuals Unlimited/Mark Gibson, 8; C. Prance, 11; Edward Hodgson, 19; Walt Anderson, 26


**Content Consultants**
Lisette Ramos
Wild Animal Keeper
Wildlife Conservation Society

Maria Kent Rowell
Science Consultant
Sebastopol, California

David Larwa
National Science Education Consultant
Educational Training Services
Brighton, Michigan

# Contents

Range of the Tamandua

Range of the Giant Anteater

Range of the Silky Anteater

Surrounding Land

Water

Borders

Rivers

N
W — E
S

**Map 1 (top)**

MEXICO
BELIZE
HONDURAS
GUATEMALA
EL SALVADOR
NICARAGUA
Caribbean Sea
COSTA RICA
PANAMA
ECUADOR
COLOMBIA
North Atlantic Ocean
VENEZUELA
GUYANA
SURINAME
FRENCH GUIANA (FRANCE)
PERU
AMAZON RIVER
BRAZIL
BOLIVIA
South Pacific Ocean
PARAGUAY
CHILE
South Atlantic Ocean
ARGENTINA
URUGUAY

**Map 2 (bottom left)**

MEXICO
BELIZE
HONDURAS
GUATEMALA
EL SALVADOR
NICARAGUA
Caribbean Sea
COSTA RICA
PANAMA
ECUADOR
COLOMBIA
North Atlantic Ocean
VENEZUELA
GUYANA
SURINAME
FRENCH GUIANA (FRANCE)
PERU
AMAZON RIVER
BRAZIL
BOLIVIA
South Pacific Ocean
PARAGUAY
CHILE
South Atlantic Ocean
ARGENTINA
URUGUAY

**Map 3 (bottom right)**

MEXICO
BELIZE
HONDURAS
GUATEMALA
EL SALVADOR
NICARAGUA
Caribbean Sea
COSTA RICA
PANAMA
COLOMBIA
ECUADOR
North Atlantic Ocean
VENEZUELA
GUYANA
SURINAME
FRENCH GUIANA (FRANCE)
PERU
AMAZON RIVER
BRAZIL
BOLIVIA
South Pacific Ocean
PARAGUAY
CHILE
South Atlantic Ocean
ARGENTINA
URUGUAY

# A Quick Look at Anteaters

## What do anteaters look like?

Most anteaters have long tails, claws, and snouts. A snout is the long front part of an animal's head, including the nose, mouth, and jaws.

## Where do anteaters live?

Anteaters live in the grassy plains and rain forests of Central and South America. Some live on the ground. Others live mostly in trees.

## What do anteaters eat?

Anteaters eat termites and ants. Some eat bees.

## Do anteaters have any enemies?

The anteater has only a few enemies. They include jaguars, mountain lions, and people. Anteaters use their strong, sharp claws to protect themselves.

Anteaters have long snouts. The snouts fit into many small places where insects live.

# Anteaters in Rain Forests

Anteaters are mammals. A mammal is a warm-blooded animal with a backbone. Warm-blooded animals have a body temperature that stays the same even when it is hot or cold outside. Temperature measures how hot or cold something is.

Anteaters have **snouts**. A snout is the long front part of an animal's head, including the nose, mouth, and jaws.

There are three kinds of anteaters. They are the giant anteater, the tamandua, and the silky anteater.

# Where Anteaters Live

Anteaters live in the **savannas** and rain forests of Central and South America. Savannas are grassy areas with few trees. Rain forests are places where many trees and plants grow close together and much rain falls.

Different kinds of anteaters live in different habitats in the savannas and forests. A habitat is a place where an animal or plant usually lives.

Giant anteaters live in swamps, rain forests, and other kinds of forests. Many live on savannas. Giant anteaters spend most of their time on the ground. They are the only anteaters that do not live in trees. They are also good swimmers.

Tamanduas live in forests and thick woodlands. Most of their time is spent in trees. They sleep and hunt in trees. During the day, they sleep in hollow tree trunks.

Silky anteaters live throughout the rain forest. They spend all of their time in trees. Their favorite home is the **kapok** tree. Kapok

> **Giant anteaters are good swimmers. They can swim around the flooded rain forest.**

trees are full of fluffy seed pods. These pods look like the fur of the silky anteater. This makes it hard for **predator**s to find the anteaters. Predators are animals that hunt and eat other animals for food. The animals that predators eat are called **prey**.

Anteaters have long, sticky tongues that can be up to 22 inches (56 cm) long.

## What Anteaters Look Like

Giant anteaters are the largest kind of anteater. They are also called great anteaters or ant bears. They can be up to 7 feet (2.1 m) long from the tip of the snout to the end of the tail. They weigh 59 to 105 pounds (22 to 39 kg).

Giant anteaters have small ears and eyes that look strange next to their long snouts. Their thin bodies are covered with stiff hair. They have bushy tails. Their tail hairs grow up to 16 inches (40.6 cm) long.

Giant anteaters have strong front legs and sharp claws. They use their claws to dig for food and to fight enemies. Their claws are 4 to 6 inches (10 to 15 cm) long. They sharpen their claws by scratching them on trees.

Giant anteaters walk on their knuckles. They tuck their claws under their feet when they walk.

Tamanduas are raccoon-sized anteaters. Tamandua is the Brazilian word for ant trap. Tamanduas are also called lesser anteaters. They are 3 to 5 feet (90 to 150 cm) long. They weigh 8 to 23 pounds (3.5 to 8.4 kg).

Tamanduas have shorter snouts, but larger ears and eyes than giant anteaters. Some of them have a thick stripe of black fur around their body and neck. Others are blonde, tan, or brown.

## The Smallest Anteaters

Silky anteaters are the smallest anteaters. They are also called pygmy anteaters, dwarf anteaters, and two-toed anteaters. They are 10 to 20 inches (25 to 50 cm) long. They weigh from 5 to 9 ounces (155 to 275 g).

Silky anteaters have silver or golden fur. Their fur is very smooth.

Silky anteaters are not as strong as other kinds of anteaters. They cannot protect themselves well, so they must hide from predators. Their **camouflage** helps them hide in kapok trees. Camouflage is colors, shapes, or patterns that make something blend in with its background.

## Tails

Tamanduas and silky anteaters have special tails. Their tails can grab and wrap around things. Tamandua tails are mostly furless.

Tamanduas and silky anteaters use their tails to move from branch to branch. Their tails also help them keep balance. They hold onto branches with their tails as they sleep.

Silky anteaters wrap their tails around tree branches. This helps them balance.

This silky anteater is sleeping. Anteaters turn food into energy as they sleep.

# Food

Anteaters are **insectivores**. An insectivore is an animal that eats only insects. Giant anteaters and tamanduas eat termites and ants. Tamanduas also sometimes eat bees. Silky anteaters eat only ants. Giant anteaters can eat 30,000 ants and termites in one day. Even the smaller silky anteaters can eat up to 5,000 insects in a day. An anteater's body changes food into energy very slowly. This is why they sleep for most of the day.

Giant anteaters spend their days on the ground looking for food. They try to find termites and ants living together in large groups.

## Termites and Ants

Groups of termites live in mounds that can be 12 feet (4 m) tall. Millions of termites live in one mound. Many ants build nests underground that are even larger than termite mounds. Some ant nests are as large as a football field.

Giant anteaters have strong senses of smell. They hold their snouts close to the ground when they walk. They move slowly. They sniff until they find ant nests. Anteaters can smell 40 times better than a person.

Giant anteaters use their sharp claws to get inside ant nests and termite mounds. They make a hole in the nest or mound. They put their snouts in the hole and lick up the ants. They also use their claws and tongues to capture ants and termites.

Other kinds of anteaters hunt in trees. There are many ants and termites in the trees. They cover the branches and leaves.

Anteaters eat termites that live in large termite mounds like this one.

This anteater is sticking its snout into the ground to look for insects.

# Eating

An anteater's tongue is long and sticky and moves very fast. They catch insects by flicking their tongues at them.

Anteaters have no teeth. They mash their food against the sides and roofs of their mouths. This helps to grind the food. When anteaters swallow their food, they also swallow sand and small stones. These bits help crush food inside an anteater's stomach.

Anteaters never ruin a nest or termite mound. If they did, they would not be able to eat from it again. Anteaters eat from many different nests and mounds. That gives insects time to mate and have more young.

Anteaters have large, curved front claws. The claws make it impossible for anteaters to walk on the bottoms of their front feet. To walk, they fold their claws in and step on the thick pad on the outsides of their front feet.

Female tamanduas give off a strong smell when they are ready to mate.

# An Anteater's Life Cycle

Anteaters live and hunt alone. The only time they get together with other anteaters is to mate, or to have young.

Mating begins when a female anteater gives off a strong scent. The tamandua's scent is especially strong. People call the female tamandua the stinker of the forest. Male anteaters smell the scent. The male finds the female, and they mate.

Giant anteaters can mate anytime during the year. The anteaters spend a lot of time together before mating. But after mating, the male leaves. Young are born in about 190 days.

## Tamanduas and Silky Anteaters

Tamanduas usually mate in the fall. The male and female leave each other after they mate. Young are born after about 140 days. Like the female giant anteater, the female tamandua raises her young on her own.

Silky anteaters are different from other kinds of anteaters. They stay together after they mate. Both males and females raise their young.

## Young

Female anteaters give birth to one anteater cub. The cub climbs onto its mother's back right away. It spends six to nine months there. On its mother's back, the cub is safe from predators.

Cubs drink their mother's milk. They also eat ants. When their mother finds an ant nest, the cub eats any ants it can catch.

Cubs leave their mothers after six to nine months. They find food on their own, but they stay close to their mothers. If there is danger, they can find their mothers quickly.

The silky anteater below is frightened. When frightened, all anteaters stand on their hind legs. They use their tails for support. They wave their claws at whatever frightens them. These actions may scare enemies so that they will leave the anteaters alone.

Giant anteaters that live in places far from people are active during the day.

# Living with Anteaters

Anteaters stay away from people. When giant anteaters live near people, they are **nocturnal**. Nocturnal means they are active at night and sleep during the day. Giant anteaters that live away from people are active during the day.

Anteaters can help people in their homes. People sometimes use tamanduas to eat the ants and termites in their homes. People think of these insects as pests. But anteaters should not be kept as pets. People should not take them from their habitats.

> **Some people help anteaters by teaching others about them.**

## Hunting

People in South America hunt giant anteaters for their meat. People also kill them because some people believe they kill dogs and cattle. This is not true.

People also hunt giant anteaters for sport. This means that people kill them for fun.

Since anteaters are not very fast, they are easy to kill.

People kill tamanduas for their tails. Inside the tails are thick tendons. A tendon is a strong cord that joins muscles and bones together. People use these tendons to make rope. The rope is very strong.

## Saving Anteaters

Hunting is not the only danger to anteaters in the wild. Some people buy and sell them as pets. People also take away their habitats. They cut down trees in the rain forests to build homes or sell the wood. Anteaters have fewer places to live.

As the rain forests are cut down, giant anteaters are becoming **endangered**. Endangered means in danger of dying out.

Anteaters do not have young very often. If too many anteaters die, their numbers could fall quickly. If people want anteaters to live, they need to protect them and their habitats.

# Glossary

**camouflage** (KAM-uh-flahzh)—colors, shapes, and patterns that make something blend in with its background

**endangered** (en-DAYN-jurd)—in danger of dying out

**insectivore** (in-SECT-uh-vor)—an animal that eats only insects

**kapok (**KAY-pohk)—a tree in rain forests that grows fluffy seed pods

**nocturnal** (nok-TUR-nuhl)—active at night

**predator** (PRED-uh-tur)—an animal that eats other animals

**prey** (PRAY)—an animal eaten by another animal

**savanna** (suh-VAN-uh)—a large, grassy area with few trees

**snout** (SNOUT)—the long front part of an animal's head, including the nose, jaws, and mouth

# Internet Sites

**Animal Diversity Web**
http://www.animaldiversity.unmz.umich.edu/
index.html

**The Virtual Zoo—Anteaters**
http://library.advanced.org/tq-admin/day.cgi

**The World of Anteaters**
http://www.geocities.com/RainForest/Vines/
6098/Anteaters.html

# Useful Addresses

**Museum of Zoology**
University of Michigan
1109 Geddes Avenue
Ann Arbor, MI 48109-1079

**Rainforest Action Network**
221 Pine Street Suite 500
San Francisco, CA 94104

# Index